DELPHI
AND ITS HISTORY

by Professor **PIERRE AMANDRY,**
Member of the "Institut de France",
Corresponding Fellow of the British Academy,
ex-Director of the French Archaeological School of Athens

Translated by
Dr. JUDITH BINDER

With 100 pictures, plans
and reconstruction map of Delphi
(coloured in large size, folded)

"GREECE — AN ARCHAEOLOGICAL GUIDE" EDITIONS

Restored view of the Sanctuary of Apollo at Delphi (By A. Tournaire)

"GREECE – AN ARCHAEOLOGICAL GUIDE"

"DELPHI and its History"

The text titled "DELPHI and its History"
was written by Pierre Amandry.
The translation from French
was made by Dr. Judith Binder.
The captions and visiting of Delphi
were made by the editor.
The plan and the reconstruction of Delphi
were made by C. Papas
Special Photography: N. Kontos and S. Tsavdaroglou

Delphi and its History

The prehistoric age

(from the 4th to the 2nd millennium before the Christian era)

Four thousand years before the Christian era people were using the Corycian Cave, a grotto 1400 metres above sea level on the plateau of Parnassus,
two and a half hours by foot from Delphi: neolithic glazed pottery and
terracotta figurines have been discovered there. But the site of Delphi was uninhabited at that time.

More than two thousand years before the Christian era there was a settlement at Kirrha on the coast; remains of houses and graves have been found
there. But the site of Delphi was still uninhabited.

The first traces of human habitation at Delphi date to about 1400 B.C. The
settlement which developed during the course of two centuries grew up on the
site where the sanctuary of Apollo was later on, from the temple to the Cnidian Lesche and further eastward toward Castalia. The finds (mainly glazed
pottery) do not let us know whether or not there was, at this early date, a
sanctuary of some importance on the site. But there was a cult at the
sanctuary of Athena: many terracotta figurines have been found at this spot,
summarily modelled and painted idols, standing with raised arms or seated on
three-legged stools.

Around 1200 B.C. the Mycenaean settlement at Delphi was destroyed by
the catastrophe of uncertain nature and origin which put an end to the feudal
society of the Achaeans, the memory of which was revived in the Homeric
epics four or five hundred years later.

The site of Delphi was not abandoned but the meagre remains of dwellings
and graves of the years 1200 - 800 B.C. bear witness to the same general state
of impoverishment revealed by finds from all over Greece.

The beginnings of the sanctuary of Apollo
(8th and 7th centuries B.C.)

The dawn of a new spring in Delphi did not come until about 800 B.C. At this time, houses built with field stones, as in the Mycenaean era, with a hearth in a corner of the room, stood on the site later occupied by the east front of the Apollo temple. But from the 8th to the 6th century the domain of the god expanded continually, pushing the houses towards the east and west where the cemetery of the Mycenaean village lay.

Nothing has survived of the 8th century sanctuary structures; subsequent terracing of the site and other building activities have obliterated all traces. According to a tradition recorded by Pausanias in the Roman period, the first temple of Apollo was made of laurel branches, the second temple of beeswax and feathers and the third one of bronze. The recently discovered remains of the earliest temple of Apollo at Eretria give an idea of these modest structures in the form of a hut or cabin.

But the number, the variety and the technical and artistic quality of the dedications made out of bronze and dating back to the 8th century B.C. are evidence that the fame of Pythian Apollo was rapidly spreading far and wide: bronze horses from Thessaly, tripods with geometric patterns from the Peloponnesus, open-work stands with human and animal motifs from Crete etc.

What part did the oracle play in the early development of the sanctuary? It is not known if Delphi was the seat of an oracle in Mycenaean times, nor is it known when the first Pythia prophecied in Apollo's name. The oracle at Delphi is thought to have played an important role in the colonization of the south Italian coasts and Sicily which began towards the middle of the 8th century B.C. But one cannot be sure that all of the responses attributed to the oracle are authentic. The priests of Apollo who were Delphians and the Pythia who was a woman of Delphi did not have enough information about geography to give advice about the most suitable place for founding a colony. In point of fact those who were on the point of sending out a colony came to Delphi after reconnoitering on their own and after they had already chosen their site in order to ask Apollo to approve the project, to look favourably on their enterprise and to indicate the names of the divinities who should have cult honours in the new homeland. Even so, the oracle's function was important: the very fact that it **was** consulted makes it sufficiently clear that at this time the sanctuary of Apollo Pythios was recognized as the religious centre of the Greek world.

In the course of the 7th century B.C. the bronze dedications became more numerous: Cretan shields, Corinthian helmets, cauldrons with gryphon protomes, some of which were manufactured in Samos and some in the Peloponnesus, and statuettes of people. Towards the end of the 7th century B.C. Apollo and Athena, the two main divinities of Delphi, were given temples of stone with Doric colonnades, dwelling-places in their sanctuaries which were worthy of their renown. Trophonius and Agamedes were thought to have been the architects of the temple of Apollo. The sole remains of both temples is but fragmentary material which was reused in the foundations of later

The inside of a cup showing a consultation with the oracle. About 440 B.C. (Staatliche Museum, Berlin).

buildings. The statues of Cleobis and Biton, dedicated by the Argives, mark the beginning of large-scale sculpture in marble.

The golden age of the sanctuary

(from the 6th to the 4th century B.C.)

There were two important events at the beginning of the 6th century B.C.: the Amphictyonic League was established at Delphi and the Pythian Games were reorganized. The Amphictyonic league was a religious association of twelve peoples, almost all from central Greece (Thessalians and *perioikoi*, Boeotians, Locrians, Phocians), with the Ionians of Attica and Euboea and the Dorians of the Metropolis (Doris in central Greece) and of the Peloponnesus; from the very beginnings of the Amphictyonic League, whose origins are shrouded in remote antiquity, the members met at the sanctuary of Demeter at Thermopylae. Drawn by the fame of the sanctuary of Pythian Apollo the Amphictyonic league transferred its headquarters to Delphi without, however, giving up the place where it had begun: the two annual conventions in spring and autumn were held partly at Thermopylae and partly at Delphi. The first

7

act of the Amphictyonic League at Delphi was to declare a Sacred War against the town of Kirrha whose inhabitants the Delphians accused of fleecing the pilgrims from the Peloponnesus who landed there. The territory belonging to Kirrha was consecrated to Apollo and cultivation of the soil was formally prohibited; this decision of a religious nature had serious consequences politically both for the Amphictyonic League and for Delphi.

In 582 B.C. the Amphictyonic League reorganized the Pythian Games, celebrating them once every four years; they came midway between the quadrennial celebrations of the Olympic games and were equally renowned. The program included musical competitions in addition to the athletic and equestrian contests. A theatre, a stadium and a race-course, made as yet only of hard - packed earth, were fixed up. A monumental fountain with four spouts was constructed at Castalia.

Votive chapels, called treasuries, were dedicated in the sanctuary by towns in thanksgiving for a stroke of good fortune. Dedications made of precious metals or of fragile materials, such as wooden panels with ivory reliefs or

*Partial view
in the centre
of the Sanctuary
of Apollo
(of the 5th c.B.C.):
The Temple of Apollo,
the column
surmounted by a
colossal Sphinx,
votive offering of the
Naxians, the porch
of the Athenians and
the polygonal wall
(reconstruction;
P. Amandry).*

chryselephantine statues, were protected from the weather in the treasuries. Statues of marble and bronze were set up in the open air with the Naxian sphinx mounted on an Ionic column ten metres high towering above all. The fame of the oracle spread beyond the boundaries of the Greek world and it was even consulted by barbarian rulers, the most famous of whom was Croesus, king of Lydia, who sent Apollo rich offerings of gold and silver.

Croesus was the one to whom the Pythia gave an oracle, as it was told, which remained famous throughout antiquity. When the king of Lydia was planning to invade territory belonging to the kingdom of Persia, he sent to the oracle to enquire if it would be the better and preferable choice for him (according to the hieratic formula) to undertake this war. The Pythia answered that in crossing the Halys (the river which formed the boundary beten Lydia and Persia), he would destroy a great empire. Croesus interpreted this response as encouragement to go ahead and he went to war. When he was beaten he complained to the oracle of having been deceived. the Pythia vindicated herself by pointing out that he should have asked a second question in order to find

The start of the Sacred Way to the Sanctuary of Apollo: The bronze bull of the Corcyreans, the ex-voto of the Arcadians (9 statues), the statue of mounted

out if he would destroy the Persian empire or his own. Ambiguity was a part of the oracular style and ancient authors have recorded a great many responses with double meanings attributed to the Pythia. Most of these oracular responses, their obscurity heightened by poetic mannerisms, were obviously composed after the event and probably not in Delphi. In antiquity, the concept of the authenticity of an historical text did not obtain the way it does in our own day, nor was literal exactness a requirement. The most conscientious historians recreated texts of speeches given by orators or texts of decrees voted by assemblies.

The certainly authentic questions, known through inscriptions, present alternatives: would it be better to do something this way or not? Would it be better to do this or that? The Pythia's choice was limited to one of two alternatives. The undoubtedly authentic responses refer, in fact, to one of the two parts of the question. It may be that in cases where a definite answer to an embarrassing question would risk compromising the oracle's prestige there were some loopholes for the Pythia...

Little is known about the procedure for consulting the oracle. We have the information that the Pythia held forth seated on a tripod in the innermost shrine of the temple of Apollo, the adyton. The enquirer first performed a sacrifice and paid a tariff; then he was admitted into the presence of the prophetess and asked his question, no doubt orally: nothing like the lead plaques on which questions to the oracle at Dodona were inscribed has ever been found at Delphi. The traditional picture of a disheveled Pythia, foaming at the

Philopoimen and the building with Doric stoa of the Hellenistic period. Left: The round "Tholos" of Sicyon. Reconstruction, H. Pomtow.

mouth, frenziedly mouthing incoherent sounds, is due to Christian authors of the 3rd and 4th centuries, Origen and St. John Chrysostom. This picture is, to say the least, biased. The Christians thought it fair play to ridicule pagan rites as they were performed in one of the most famous pagan sanctuaries. We do not have the other side of the story: no pagan author, not even Plutarch, has described a consultation with the Pythian oracle.

But Apollo's fame had grown more quickly than his sanctuary and the offerings dedicated to him were richer than his own dwelling. In the mid-6th century B.C. a fire destroyed the temple built by Trophonius and Agamedes. The construction of a new temple, a larger and more beautiful one, brought about far-reaching changes in the sanctuary. The precinct of the god was enlarged and enclosed by a wall in polygonal masonry (still well preserved at the west): the temple itself was set off from its surroundings by a sturdy east - west retaining wall also in polygonal masonry (not covered with inscriptions until later on in the 3rd and 2nd centuries B.C.). The construction of the polygonal wall caused the destruction of some dozen earlier structures (the remains of which are still visible, built into the foundations of the the wall or buried in the terrace). The Alcmaeonids, exiled from Athens by the Peisistratids, were in charge of building the temple; they made the east front of Parian marble and the rest of Sicyonian tufa. The east pediment showed Apollo arriving at Delphi in a chariot; the west pediment had Athena battling a giant. In the same period the temple of Athena was rebuilt in her sanctuary which, in spite of its great antiquity, did not fully share in Apollo's glory. At the same time the Corycian

Cave, which had been abandoned at the end of the Neolithic period, frequented anew in the Mycenaean period and deserted a second time, now became a kind of subsidiary of the Delphic sanctuary, consecrated to Pan and the Nymphs, where less costly offerings poured in: bronze and iron rings have been found in the cave by the hundreds, terracotta figurines by the thousands.

The crisis brought on by the Persian wars very nearly tarnished the lustre of Pythian Apollo. When they had won the war the allied Greeks did not bear the oracle a grudge for the ambiguous attitude it had it had adopted before the issue of the struggle had been decided: for it was at Delphi that thirty-one peoples and towns, who had taken part in the battles of Salamis and Plataia, dedicated a golden tripod financed from the booty; the tripod was supported by a bronze column made of three entwined serpents on which they had their names engraved.

Delphi, the religious centre of the Greek world, "the central hearth of all Greece" as Pindar wrote, was also the moral centre: the Seven Wise Men (including Thales of Miletus and Solon of Athens) had maxims written in the forehall of Apollo's temple, "the most useful maxims for the conduct of life" according to Pausanias who was able to read them there in the 2nd century of our era. The most famous were "know thyself" and "nothing too much."

12

The Treasury of the Siphnians. Reconstruction, A. Tournaire.

As the crowning touch Delphi was considered to be the geographic centre of the earth: a conical stone, called omphalos (or navel), probably inherited from ancient cults, was believed to mark the spot where the two eagles met, whom Zeus had sent forth from the opposite ends of the earth to fly towards each other.

Apollo received offerings from every region of the Greek world. We know something about these offerings, thanks to the discoveries of their remains or because some of the dedicatory inscriptions have survived or because they are mentioned by ancient authors (Plutarch and Pausanias in particular). The chief towns of the mainland and the islands dedicated one or more monuments at Delphi, treasuries, stoas, statue groups: Sparta, Messeneh Mantinea, Argos, Epidaurus, Corinth, Sicyon, Megara, Athens (which adorned the sanctuary with a Doric treasury with sculptured metopes showing the deeds of Herakles and of Theseus and with an Ionic stoa built against the polygonal wall), Aegina, Carystus, Thebes (a treasury commemorating the victory at the battle of Leuctra in 373 B.C., built in grey limestone from the quarries of St. Elias between Delphi and Amphissa), Plataea, Pharsalus, Dion, Potidaea, Ambracia, Corcyra, Siphnos (the Siphnian Treasury made out of marble, with Caryatids instead of columns and with sculptured friezes, was one of the most

beautiful monuments of archaic architecture and sculpture), Naxos, Rhodes, Samos, Chios (which gave the altar in front of the temple to Apollo). Offerings were also sent from towns on the coasts of Asia Minor and the Black Sea (Knidos, Klazomenae, Heraclea), from African colonies (Cyrene), from Magna Graecia and Sicily (Tarentum, Lipari, Syracuse), from Etruria (Caere), from Gaul (Massalia which dedicated a treasury in the sanctuary of Athena). This list is far from exhaustive.

The golden tripod supported by a statue of Victory, dedicated at Delphi by Gelon after his victory over the Carthiginians in 480 B.C., can be taken to symbolize Delphi's position as the central hearth of Hellenism and the meeting - place for the Greek West and the Greek East: the tripod was the work of an Ionian artist, Bion of Miletus; the donor's dedication on the monument base is written in the Corinthian alphabet (Corinth was the mother-city of Syracuse) followed by the artist's signature in the Ionian alphabet. Hieron, Gelon's younger brother, gave another tripod. After his team won in the Pythian games, a third brother, Polyzalos, dedicated a bronze chariot of which only the charioteer survives. Gelon and Hieron had also won victories in the hippodrome at Olympia and had had similar groups made for the Altis, carried

14

The Treasury of the Athenians. Reconstruction, A. Tournaire.

out by famous sculptors, Glaukias, Onatas, Calamis. At the same time they had poets celebrate their victories with triumphal odes. Pindar's *Olympian Odes* and *Pythian Odes* were, like the statues, commissioned works.

In comparison with the large-scale sculpture in marble, bronze, gilded wood and ivory, the statuettes seem like poor relations. Nonetheless they are by no means of inferior quality: for instance, the girl wearing a peplos, holding an incense-burner in her upraised hands, stands up to comparison with the Charioteer.

Between 380 - 360 B.C. the sanctuary of Athena, which had been somewhat neglected in the 5th century B.C., was embellished with two monuments: the marble Tholos with sculptured metopes (we do not know why the Tholos was built) and a new temple of Athena made out of St. Elias limestone.

The temple of Apollo also had to be rebuilt because the temple which the Alcmaeonids had erected at the end of the 6th century B.C. was partially destroyed in 373 B.C., probably by an earthquake. The rebuilding of the temple provided the Delphic sanctuary with a new opportunity (its last one) to demonstrate its panhellenic character. The Amphictyonic League levied con-

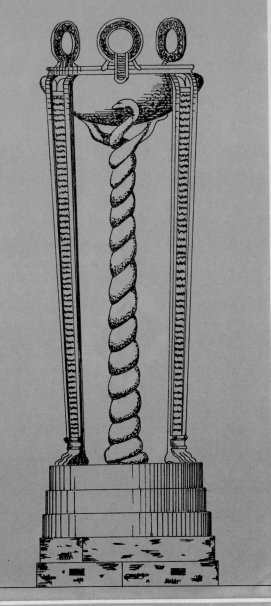

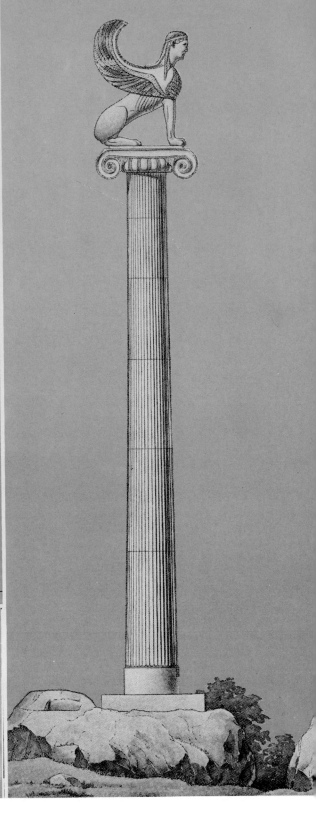

Left: The golden tripod of Plataea (reconstruction, K. Papas) and the column with the Sphinx of the Naxians (reconstruction, A. Tournaire).
Right: The column with three dancers (reconstruction, M. Evrard and I. Athanassiadou) and the statue of mounted Harixenos (reconstruction, S. de Fonseca).

The bronze sculpture group of the Charioteer. Reconstruction, E. Krischen.

tributions and collected donations throughout the Mediterranean coastal areas; a committee was formed to administer the funds. The platform and orthostates of the new temple (the ruins of which are what one sees now) were built of limestone from the St. Elias quarries, the walls and columns were of tufa from Sicyon.

But religion and politics were so inextricably intertwined in ancient Greece that it was not possible for the Delphic sanctuary to avoid being affected by quarrels between cities. In the 5th and 4th centuries B.C. the monuments presented to Apollo sometimes commemorated the victory of a coalition of Greeks against barbarians (but the names of the Thessalians, the Thebans and the Argives, among others, were missing on the column under the Tripod of Plataea), sometimes a victory of western Greek colonists over natives, but more often a victory of Greeks against Greeks. Plutarch was exasperated when he read the dedications on these monuments: they commemorated wars between Athens and Sparta, between Argos and Sparta, between Athens and Corinth, between Thebes and Sparta, between Arcadians and Spartiates, between Phocians and Thessalians, between the Amphictyonic League and the Phocians.

These conflicts amongst Greeks were to reach a climax, by an ironical twist of fate, in a Sacred War decreed by the Amphictyonic League and originating in the panhellenic sanctuary itself. The remains of the Alcmaeonid temple had been dismantled block by block and the material had been reused to erect a retaining wall (called *ischegaon* in the texts) to the north of the temple terrace and to reinforce the foundations of the new temple at the west, and the temple had already started to go up, when a dispute broke out between local clans, and neighbouring districts fanned the flames of the quarrel; the one side accused the other of having cultivated a part of the territory of Kirrha which was under a curse, which in turn provoked the Amphictyonic League into interven-

18

The bronze sculpture group of Alexander the Great. Reconstruction, F. Courby.

ing and declaring a Sacred War against the Phocians whose territory included Delphi. The war lasted ten years, from 356 - 346 B.C. The Phocian chieftains robbed the sanctuary of Apollo of all offerings made of precious metals (craters of gold and silver given by Croesus, Gelon's golden tripod, the golden tripod of Plataea etc.), melted them down and minted money in order to pay mercenary soldiers. Philipp of Macedon put his army at the disposition of the Amphictyonic League to which he was admitted in place of the sacrilegious Phocians when they had been defeated. Then, intervening once more under the pretext of upholding Apollo's interests, Philipp put an end to the differences between the Greek city-states by forcing them to accept him as overlord, in spite of a desperate attempt of the Thebans and Athenians, whom Demosthenes had reconciled at the last minute, to halt the advance of the Macedonian army at Chaeronea in 338 B.C.

The building of the temple of Apollo, at first slowed down, then halted by the Sacred War, was finished during the years following the cessation of hostilities, thanks to the resources provided by the penalties imposed on the Phocians.

The last treasury in the sanctuary, given by the colonists of Cyrene, was also completed during the reign of Alexander the Great. The main structures of the gymnasium likewise date from this period.

The portrait of the conquering Macedonian was set up in the sanctuary of Apollo, near to the temple, in a niche opened up for the purpose in the ischegaon: a bronze sculpture group, the work of Leochares, showed Alexander being rescued from an attacking lion by one of his officers, Craterus, during the campaign in Asia. Craterus' son dedicated this work in memory of his father.

That was an entirely new thing. Up until that point individual offerings coming from barbarian rulers, such as Croesus, or Greek tyrants, such as Gelon

19

and Hieron, were thought of as dedicated in the name of the people or cities they governed. An offering from a private person was something exceptional even on the part of the victors of the Pythian games. Ancient authors mention dedications by courtesans, such as Rhodopis' brooches or the statue of Phryne, sometimes as a matter for indignation. Private dedications had become customary by the end of Alexander's era. For example, Daochos, the chief magistrate of the Thessalian town of Pharsalus, dedicated nine marble statues representing six generations of his family; the statues were all on one base and the statue of his greatgrandfather, Agias, who had won the wrestling match at the Olympic games, was a replica of a statue by Lysippus which Daochos had set up in Pharsalus. It is not known whether a town or a private person set up the acanthus column beside the Thessalian monument; at the top of the column were three dancers who supported a tripod, just as a Victory suppor- ted the cauldron of Gelon's tripod and the serpent column supported the cauldron of the tripod of the Plataeans.

The sanctuary in the 3rd and 2nd centuries B.C.

Alexander's conquests had carried Hellenism to the remote parts of India, Mesopotamia and Nubia. In the 3rd century B.C. the kingdoms which emerged from the break-up of Alexander's empire had their capital cities in Macedonia, Asia Minor, Syria, Egypt. On the other side of the Mediterranean the Romans conquered Italy and Sicily, including Tarentum, Syracuse, and the other Greek towns, before going on to Africa and Greece itself. The old towns of Greece - Athens, Sparta, Corinth, Thebes - no longer played a political role in this new world. Delphi, centre of a world of disintegrating city- states, suffered inevitable changes.

But there were still donors who seized the opportunity of displaying their power or their vainglory by making dedications to Pythian Apollo. On mainland Greece those who now held power were the ones who had previous- ly been on the sidelines or lived in obscurity: the Achaeans, the Aetolians, the Epirotes, the Macedonians. In the 3rd century B.C. the Aetolians extended their sway to Locris and Phocis and became masters of Delphi. They set up monuments there: a large stoa west of the sanctuary to display armour cap- tured from the Galatians, a statue of Aetolia personified, statues of their generals. A new theatre and a new stadium probably date to this time. There were numerous offerings made by individual Aetolians, among them are at least four monuments of a novel type, two of them given by women: two Ionic columns supporting an entablature serving as a pedestal for a statue of the dedicator or a member of the family.

Amongst the Hellenistic sovereigns the kings of Pergamon were the most munificent, dividing their bounty between Athens and Delphi. They sent money and workmen for the maintenance of the sanctuary of Pythian Apollo. Attalos I commemorated his victory over the Galatians (who invaded Asia Minor after they had been driven out of Greece) by building a monumental complex to the east of the temple for which a part of the sanctuary precinct wall had to be demolished; the complex included a vaulted chamber, a stoa (later turned into a cistern) and a long base with statues on it.

In return the kings of Pergamon received honours from the Amphictyonic

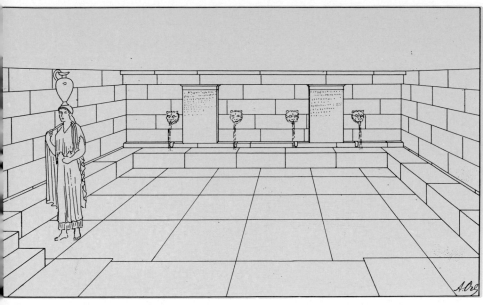

The Castalia fountain of the archaic period. Reconstruction, A. Orlandos.

League and from the Aetolians: statues of Attalos I and Eumenes II were mounted on high shafts set up at the approach to the front of the temple. A statue of Prusias II, king of Bithynia was set up in the same way (the pillar for this statue has been reerected). Another pillar must have supported the statue of Perseus, the last king of Macedonia; the Roman general, Aemilius Paulus, who defeated Perseus, replaced Perseus' statue with his own.

Delphi has a wealth of inscriptions carved during this period. The walls of buildings and even the great polygonal wall are covered with inscriptions. A great many of the inscriptions are honorary decrees granted by the town of Delphi or by the Amphictyonic League, which are extremely long-winded by comparison with the brevity of texts written in earlier centuries (which were usually carved on marble stelai like the one still in place in front of the base of Gelon's tripod). There are also many inscriptions recording the manumission of slaves; Apollo guaranteed that when a slave had finished paying out the price he would be set free. A special record concerning the Pythais was carved on the Athenian Treasury; the Pythais was a procession which the Athenians sent to Delphi when they received a divine signal, lightning striking a particular place on Mount Parnes. One may read there texts about artists' associations and the text of a hymn to Apollo with musical notation between the lines.

The decline of the sanctuary

(from the 1st century B.C. to the 3rd century of our era)

After the close of the civil wars amongst the Romans which came to an end on Greek soil at Philippi in 42 B.C. and in Greek waters, at Actium, in 31 B.C., Greece, now reduced to the status of a province in the Roman empire, experienced the joys of peace for more than two hundred years, something

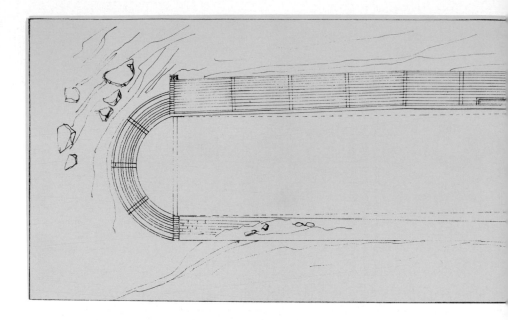

which had been virtually unknown throughout the long history of the country. But intellectual and artistic activity slowed down along with political life and Delphi did not escape the prevalent atmosphere of drowsiness.

The theatre was decorated with a frieze of mediocre quality, representing the labours of Hercules. A rock - cut fountain with façade and collecting basin was hewn out of the Castalian gorge. But there were no funds for the upkeep of the sanctuary; weeds pushed their way between wall blocks and roof timbers rotted away. In the first century of our era a fire damaged the temple of Apollo; Domitian had the temple repaired at his expense, if one is to believe the monumental inscription commemorating his imperial bounty.

The *Pythian Dialogues* by Plutarch, who was the priest of Apollo and epimelete of the Amphictyons at the end of his long life, in the first quarter of the 2nd century, gives an impression of neglect, a picture of the end of a world; one catches the scent of faded flowers and mouldiness. The Amphictyonic Council continued to convene; it organized Pythian games; it voted honorary decrees and set up statues of Roman consuls or emperors. The oracle was still being consulted. But where were the days of yesteryear when the mighty of the earth came to ask the oracle before making an alliance or going to war? Plutarch says that the oracle was now consulted only about a sea voyage or about a marriage!

Yet in the 2hd century under the Antonines, Delphi had one last flash of brilliance, a pale reflection of vanished glory. The Roman emperors corresponded with the town of Delphi; the text of their letters - of which the latest dates to 221 A.D. in the reign of Heliogabulus - was carved on the orthostates of the temple of Apollo. Hadrian visited Delphi twice. The Delphians had a statue of Antinous set up in the sanctuary of Apollo (it has been found), after the emperor's favourite had drowned himself in the Nile.

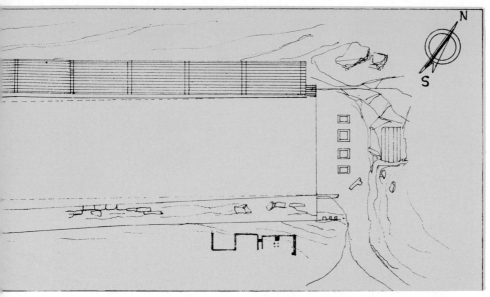

*The **Stadium of Delphi.** Plan, K. Papas.*

The rich sophist, Herodes Atticus, patron of literature and the arts, lavished his donations on Athens, Olympia and on Delphi where he had the seats of the stadium rebuilt in Hag. Elias stone and set up statues of members of his family in the ancient sanctuary of Ge (Earth) in front of the great polygonal wall.

Although the Pythian sanctuary still had visitors, they were more often curiousity seekers than believers. After Plutarch's friends had learnedly discussed philosophical problems in front of the temple of Apollo, they climbed up to the plateau on Mount Parnassus to see the Corycian Cave just as tourists do today. Fifty years later when Pausanias visited the sanctuary at Delphi in order to describe the monuments, he came as an historian enquiring about the antiquities: Agamemnon was as far distant from him as Charlemagne is from us and the Parthenon from a Romanesque church.

The Phocians had earlier despoiled the sanctuary of its gold and silver offerings and a number of statues were removed by those great amateurs of Greek art, Sulla and Nero. But we know that there were still many statues remaining in the 2nd century because Plutarch and his friends discussed the origin of the patina on statues which they saw around them and Pausanias, too, saw and mentioned a great number of statues.

But a century and a half later when Constantine wanted to adorn the capital of the empire in the east to which he gave his name, he took nothing from Delphi except for the serpent column which still stood in place useless and forlorn ever since the Phocians had removed the golden tripod seven hundred years ago. Did Constantine deliberately overlook the thirty-seven bronze statues dedicated by the Spartans after the victory at Aegospotami, the sixteen statues commemorating the Athenian victory at Marathon, the nine statues of the Arcadians, the twenty-five statues of the Argives, the twenty statues of Apollo given by the Liparians, the statue groups of the Tarentines, Boeotians,

23

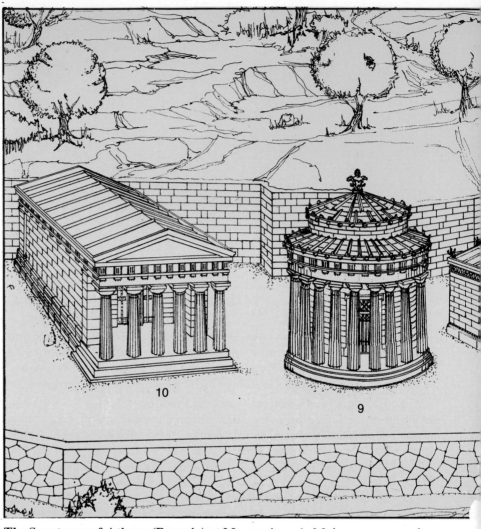

10

9

The Sanctuary of Athena (Pronaia) at Marmaria. *1. Main entrance to the
Sanctuary (from the east). 1a. Present entrance (from the north).   2. The
Delphic Heroön (?).   3. Altars.   4. The porous-stone Temple of Athena.
About 510 B.C.   5. Doric Trēasury. About 470 B.C.   6. Ionic Treasury*

Phocians, Apollo Sitalkas 35 cubits high and dozens of other statues? Or, as is
more likely, had they all disappeared since Pausanias saw them? In the 3rd
century a wave of barbarian invasions swept through Greece. The Herulians,
the Goths, the Bastarnae overran central Greece, Attica, the Peloponnesus,
plundering and burning as they went Did they overturn the statues and smash
them to bits? Or did it happen after the edict of Theodosius, a century later
when the Delphians themselves furiously attacked pagan idols, melting the
bronze gods into ingots and burning the marble gods in the limekilns? We will
never know. In any case, they have almost all disappeared. How many of the
hundreds of the statues that once populated the sanctuary have survived? The

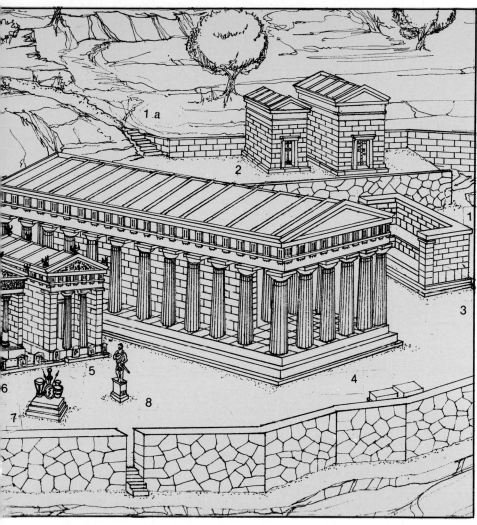

- of the Massiliotes. About 520 B.C.   7. Delphic Trophy. About 480
B.C.   8. Statue of the emperor Hadrian. About 128 A.C.   9. The Tholos.
About 380 B.C.   10. The stone Temple of Athena. About 360 B.C.
Reconstruction, K. Papas.

pediment sculpture of the Alcmaeonid temple, the Charioteer, the silver bull,
the fragments of chryselephantine works have been recovered because they
were damaged by accidents in antiquity and were buried in the ground within
the sanctuary before it was plundered, just as the korai on the Acropolis were
buried after the Persian invasion.

The end of the cult of Apollo and the triumph of Christianity
(from the 4th to the 6th century)

Not only did the statues disappear but monuments were thrown down. By
the hand of man or by an earthquake? The fact remains that the destruction

The Tholos in the sanctuary of Athena (Pronaia) at Marmaria. On the right the poros-stone temple of Athena. (Reconstruction; K. Courby).

had made powerful inroads by the time the so-called Sacred Way was paved; the entire paving consists of blocks deriving from ancient monuments, some with inscriptions, others with remains of the clamps and dowels by means of which blocks had been fastened together; fragments of several structures from the sanctuary have even been found underneath the paving stones. The road paved in the manner just described was the street for the little town which settled into the half-ruined sanctuary. Since the Athenian Treasury was still standing the money-changers used it for their transactions: their names are inscribed on the walls.

There was still a priest of Apollo a little before the middle of the 4th century. Was the oracle still working then? Around 360 A.D. the Emperor Julian had sent an emissary to the oracle who is supposed to have given this response:

> Tell the king the fairwrought hall has fallen to the ground
> No longer has Apollo a hut, nor a prophetic laurel
> Nor a spring that speaks. The water of speech even is quenched.
> (translated by H.W. Parke)

This response is apocryphal, perhaps invented by the Christians, but nonetheless it reflects a real situation: the Delphians probably did not wait until

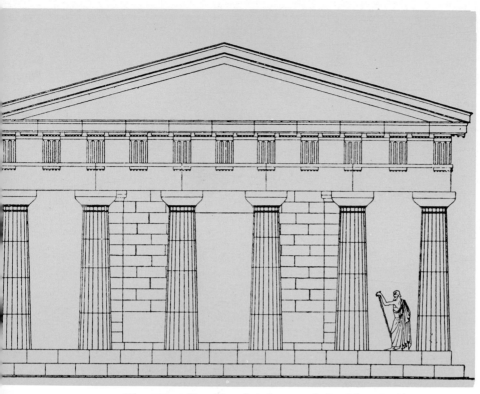

*The stone Temple of Athena, of the 4th c.B.C.
(reconstruction, J-P. Michaud - J. Blécon).*

392 A.D., when Theodosius ordered the temples closed, to take possession, at least partially, of Apollo's domain.

In the 5th century Delphi was the seat of a bishopric. Churches went up in the old sanctuary of Apollo; marble blocks from pagan monuments were used as building material, particularly blocks from the Cnidian Treasury on which the cross was carved. (Most of the remains of Christian architecture, from all parts of the site, have been collected in the so-called Roman Agora). A large basilica was built on the site where the village is now (mosaics from the nave are on show in front of the museum).

The town of Delphi entered a period of prosperity marked by the construction of important buildings made of brick and rubble, especially bathing establishments: baths were built in the Stoa of the Aetolians, in the niche of the Craterus Monument, below the Stoa of Attalos (which was made into a reservoir) and near the Castalia fountain. The so-called Roman Agora, stoas containing shops around a paved esplanade in front of the entrance to the ancient Apollo sanctuary, was also probably built at this time. One may visualize the Christian town of Delphi nestling in the ruins of the sanctuary of Apollo like the far grander Renaissance buildings in the ruins of Roman forums or the palace of Diocletian at Split, or like modern structures in the precinct of the temple of Bel at Palmyra or, in Athens itself, in the Library of Hadrian.

But the threat of Slavic invasions began to cast a shadow, The town of

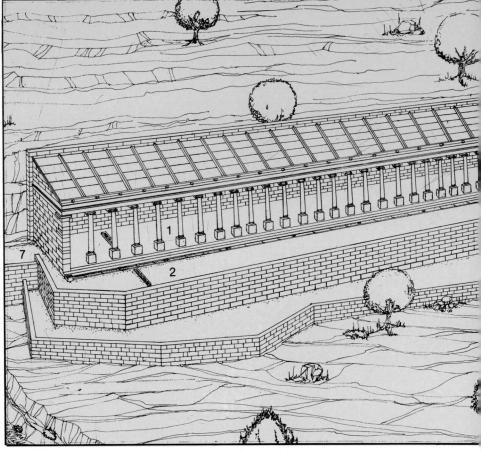

The Cymnasium of Delphi - *of the Roman period: 1. Stoa (covered track—xystos). 2. Track (paradromis). 3. Cold bath. 4. Palaestra.*

Delphi was now protected by a city wall; the gymnasium was inside the wall but the ruins of the sanctuary of Athena were outside. The date (6th or 7th century), the circumstances and the exact nature of the catastrophe which befell Delphi are unkown. The churches and the baths were destroyed as had been the pagan temples and dedications before them.

The Middle Ages and after

The site was probably not completely deserted. Graves, dug out even inside the ancient sanctuary of Apollo, covered with marble slabs taken from churches (chancel plaques) or from pagan buildings (metopes from the Treasury of the Athenians), are evidence that the place was still inhabited although to a much lesser extent. Delphi was now just a poor village like others and had ceased to be a part of history.

Little by little the ruins were buried under soil and stones washed down by the rains and pieces of rock which broke off from the Phaedriades every once and so often. Nonetheless there were some ancient remains still to be seen in

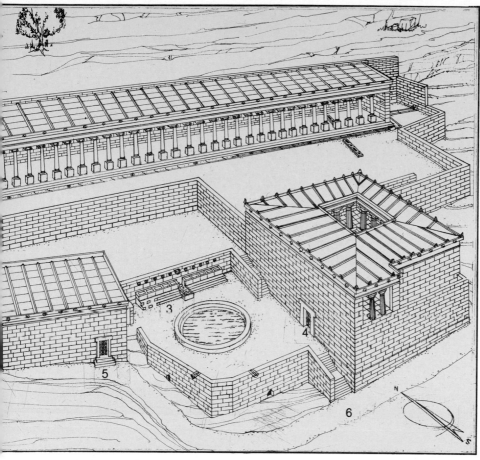

5. Hot bath.   6. Entrance (from the Sanctuary of Athena Pronaia).
7. Entrance (from the Castalian Spring). Reconstruction, K. Papas.

the 15th century when Cyriacus of Ancona copied the texts of inscriptions at Delphi. But in the 17th century people were not even certain anymore where the sanctuary of Apollo was: it was often located at Amphissa. In 1676 two travellers, the Frenchman Jacques Spon and the Englishman George Wheler, removed all doubts about the identification of the site by reading the name Delphi in ancient inscriptions to be seen in a monastery church built on the walls of the gymnasium and in the houses of the village called Kastri which occupied the site of the sanctuary of Apolo.

The excavations

After the site of Delphi had been rediscovered, two centuries elapsed before anyone undertook to dig out the ruins. In 1840 the German archaeologist Karl Otfried Müller cleared the eastern end of the great polygonal wall in the midst of the village houses of Castri; he died of a fever contracted there. From 1860 to 1862 Paul Foucart and Carl Wescher, members of the École française d'Athènes (founded in 1846) conducted three excavation campaigns; they

cleared the western section of the polygonal wall to a length of 40 metres and transcribed the inscriptions written on the wall. In 1880 Bernard Haussoullier was able to extend the excavation of 1840; he found the Athenian Stoa and a section of the so-called Sacred Way.

But the village on the site hindered any attempt at a thorough investigation. In 1891 the governments of Greece and France signed an agreement. Thanks to an extraordinary grant voted by the French parliament it was possible to expropriate the entire village and rebuild it at its present site. The excavations began in 1892 under the direction of Théophile Homolle. The investigation of the sanctuary of Apollo lasted until 1897. The ruins of Castalia, the gymnasium and the sanctuary of Athena were cleared in 1898 - 1904.

After this period of concentrated activity the French School devoted itself to the supplementary work required for the study and publication of earlier discoveries. In 1938-1939 new important discoveries were made when the paving stones of the so-called Sacred Way were taken up: fragments of chryselephantine statues - with faces, hands, and feet of ivory and hair of gold - and the silver-plated bull were found in trenches, where the wooden cores for the bodies of the statues had rotted away; they had been buried there at the end of the 5th century B.C.

At the same time some restorations were put in hand. These projects had to

progress. South side of the Sanctuary of Apollo in 1893 (By A. Tournaire)

be carried out with the utmost caution after a painstaking study of all existing remains. In 1905 the Treasury of the Athenians was restored by the French School aided by a grant from the city of Athens. The partial restoration of the temple of Apollo (1939 and 1950) and the Tholos in the sanctuary of Athena (1938) and the reconstruction of the Pillar of Prusias (1947) was carried out by the French School at the expense of the French government. The Greek Archaeological Service has carried out restorations at the Castalian fountain (1958), in the so-called Roman Agora (1978) and on the Chian altar (1958).

Eight more or less complete columns of the archaic temple of Athena, which had been consolidated or reerected soon after the ruins of the temple had been cleared, were crushed by two great boulders in the landslide of 1905; these boulders, which up until recently had survived in place, remind us of the other accidents which befell the monuments of Delphi over the course of centuries.

Catastrophes from natural causes have destroyed or damaged monuments in the sanctuary of Apollo over and over again; the damage has been repaired each time, thanks to the devotion of anonymous friends or to the (occasionally ostentatious) generosity of sovereigns. The Pythian sanctuary escaped looting by Persians and Galatians; it suffered to an immeasurable degree under the incursions of the Maedi in the first century B.C. and the Herulians and Bastar-

31

nae in the 3rd century of our era. Sulla and Nero robbed the sanctuary of artworks. But above all political quarrels and religious fanaticism were fatal to the sanctuary.

The museum at Delphi is one of the richest museums in Greece. Cleobis and Biton, the Naxian sphinx, the Caryatids and the friezes of the Siphnian Treasury, the pediment sculpture of the Alcmaeonid temple, the metopes from the Athenian Treasury and from the Tholos, the Charioteer, the Dancers, Agias, Antinous, what kind of picture of Delphi can all this sculpture convey in comparison with the three hundred statues which Pausanias was still able to see? One has to make an effort to imagine the mass of statues - standing in the open air on bases, on columns, on pillars, or sheltered under stoa colonnades - the dazzling whiteness of Parian or Pentelic marble, light reflected from gilded bronze, in the midst of temples and treasuries with friezes painted blue and bright red, at the foot of the Phaedriades cliffs, looking out over the bluish shadows of Kirphis, the grey expanse of olive trees and the indigo patch of the bay of Kirrha.

Pierre AMANDRY

Silver stater of the Delphic Amphictyonic League, about 338 B.C.
A facing: Demeter head. On the reverse, the Apollo on the Omphalos

The remains of the sanctuary of Apollo at Delphi. (Air view).

DELPHI

PLAN OF THE SANCTUARY OF APOLLO

1. Court and stoa :
   agora (market place) of the Roman period.
2. Main entrance of the Sacred Way
   to the Sanctuary of Apollo.
3. Bronze bull. Votive offering of the Corkyrans.
   About 480 B.C.
4. The Admirals of the Spartans (37 statues).
   About 404 B.C.
5. Ex-voto of the Arcadians (9 statues).
   About 371 B.C.
6. Statue of mounted Philopoimen.
   About 207 B.C.
7. Stoa of the Hellenistic period.
8. Ex-voto of the Athenians to commemorate
   their victory at Marathon, composed of 13
   statues, created by Phidias. About 460 B.C.
9-10-11-12. Argive votive monuments :
9. Bronze «Dourian Horse» (Wooden Horse of
   Troy). About 371 B.C.
10. Statues of the «Seven against Thebes».
    About 456 B.C.
11. Statues of «Epigones». About 456 B.C.
12. The Kings of Argos (10 statues).
    About 369 B.C.
13. Ex-voto of the Tarentines. About 473 B.C.
14. Treasury of the Sikyonians. 6th c. B.C.
15. Statues of the Knidians. 6th c.B.C.
16. Votive offering of the Aitolians. 3rd c.B.C.
17. Treasury of the Siphnians. 530 B.C.
18. Ex-voto of the Liparians.
19. Treasury of the Thebans. About 371 B.C.
20. Treasury of the Beotians. 6th c.B.C.
21. The Omphalos (navel-stone) - present position.
22. Treasury of the Poteidaians.
23. Treasury of the Athenians: 590-585 B.C.
24. Treasury of the Syracusans. About 413 B.C.
25. Treasury of the Megarians.
26. Aiolian Treasury - of the Klazomens.
27. Treasury of the Knidians. 6th c.B.C.
28. Pedestals and bases of monuments.
29. The polygonal wall. 6th c.B.C.
30. The Delphic Council House (Bouleuterion).
31. Ex-voto of the Boeotians.
32. The Asklepieion and spring.
33. Pedestal of Herod Atticus.
34. The Sanctuary of the goddess Ge (Earth) and
    the Muses. Kassotis Spring (6th c.B.C.).
35. Spring of the Sanctuary of the goddess Ge.
36. The column (10m.) surmounted by a colossal
    Sphinx. Votive offering of the Naxians.
    570 B.C.
37. The rock of Sibyl.
38. The rock of Leto.
39. The Halos : threshing floor.
40. Treasury of the Kyreneans. 4th c.B.C.
41. The Delphic Prytanaion (Magistrates' Hall).
42. Treasury of the Corinthians. 6th c.B.C.
43. Porch of the Athenians. About 478 B.C.
44. Treasury of the Akanthians. About 422 B.C.
45. Ex-voto of the Tarentines.
46. Golden tripod with serpent column. Ex-voto
    of the Greeks victors the Persians at the Battle
    of Plataea in 479 B.C.
47. Columns of the Messenians. About 425 B.C.
48. Statue of Aemilius Paulus. 168 B.C.
49. Altar of Apollo, erected by the Chans.
    6th c.B.C.
50. Stele of Cleitor (Arkadia). 332 B.C.
51. Tripods and Victories of gold, offered by the
    Syracusans sons of Deinomenes, Gelon and
    Hieron after the victory at Himera over the
    Carthaginians. About 479 B.C.
52. The golden chariot of Helios, dedicated by
    the Rhodians. About 304 B.C.
53. The Stoa of Attalos I. 3rd c.B.C.
54. Building (oikos) of Attalos.
55. Monument of Attalos I, King of Pergamon.
56. Statue of Attalos I.
57. Statue of Eumenes II.
58. Archaic Treasury.
59. Ex-voto of Corkyrans.
60. Column with three dancers. 325 B.C.
61. The temenos with shrine of Neoptolemos,
    son of Achilleus.
62. The Thessalian monument, build
    by Daochos II. About 335 B.C.
63. Votive offering, from the Hellenistic period.
64. The Charioteer. Most likely position.
    About 470 B.C.
65. Statues of the generals of Aitolians.
    About 279 B.C.
66. Spring of Cassotis (4th c.B.C.).
67. Column with statue of Prusias.
68. The bronze Palm Tree, surmounted by a gilt
    statue of Athena. Votive offering of the Athe-
    nians after their victory over the Persians near
    the Eurymedon River won in 468 B.C.
69. Ex-voto of Aristaineta.
70. Colossal statue of Apollo Sitalkas.
71. Column that carried a statue of Eumenes II,
    King of Pergamon. 2nd c.B.C.
72. The Temple of Apollo. Reconstruction of the
    Temple of the 6th c.B.C.
73. Pedestals of statues.
74. Western Portico - of Aitolians. 3rd c.B.C.
75. Archaic Treasury.
76. The lion hunt of Alexander the Great -
    a bronze group. Monument consecrated
    by Crateros. About 320 B.C.
77. The stage building of the Theatre.
78. The Theatre of Delphi.
79. Archaic Treasuries.
80. The rock of Cronos.
81. Lesche (meeting hall) of the Cnidians.
    About 460 B.C.
82. Exit towards Stadium.

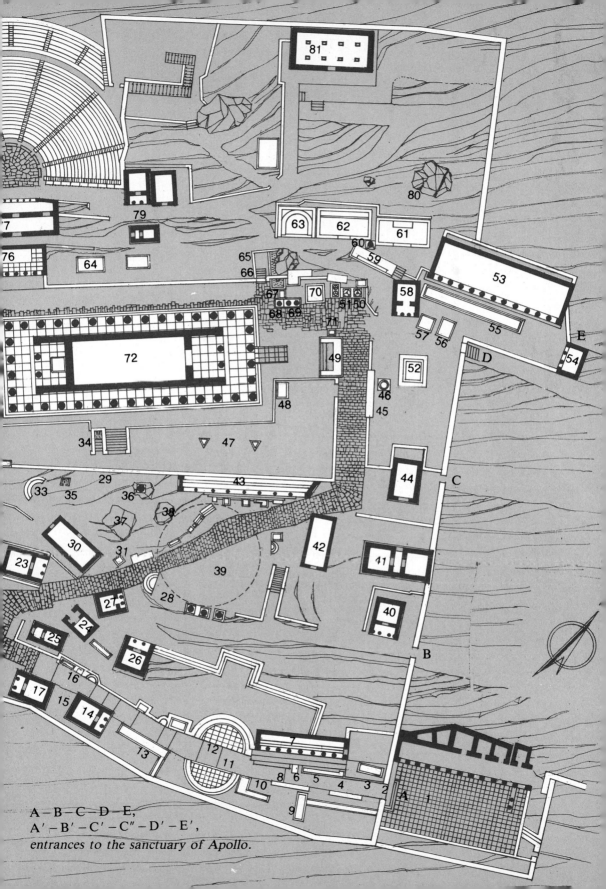

81

7

79

76

80

63 62 61

59

65
66

60

53

67
68 69

70

51 50

58

57 56

55

E

64

71

49

52

D

54

72

46

45

48

34

47

44

C

33 35

29

43

31

42

41

B

36

30

37

38

39

28

40

23

27

24

25

26

16

17

15

14

13

12 11

7

10

8 6 5 4 3 2 A 1

9

A – B – C – D – E,
A′ – B′ – C′ – C″ – D′ – E′,
entrances to the sanctuary of Apollo.

DELPHI MUSEUM

Ground plan of the 1st floor. Exhibits are indicated by numbers.

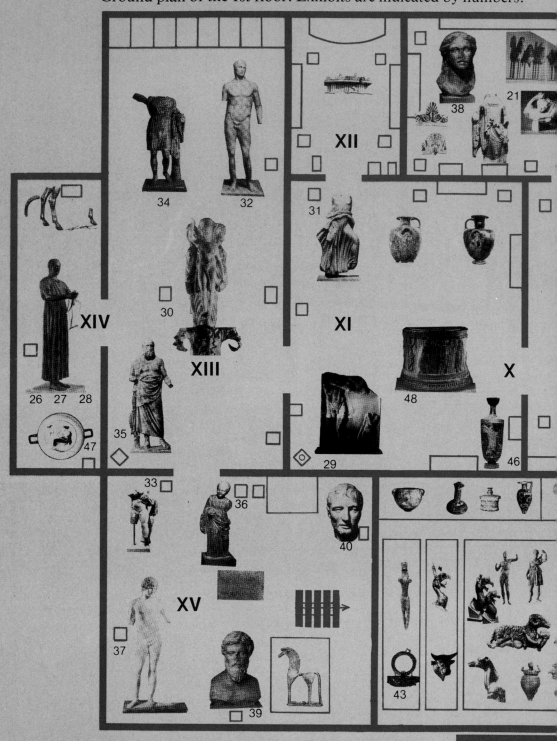

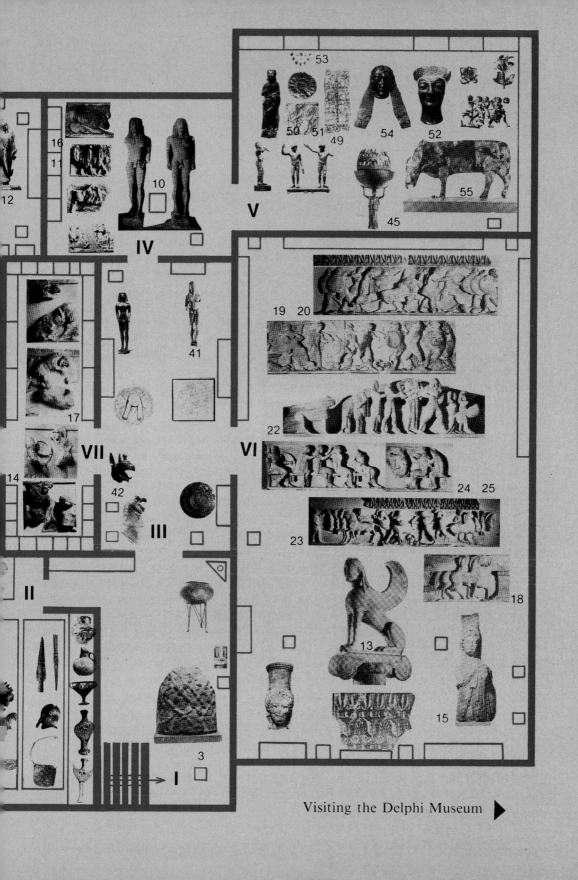

16
11

12

10

IV

V

53

50 51 49

54 52

55

45

19 20

41

22

VII

42

17

14

III

VI

24 25

23

18

13

II

15

3

I

Visiting the Delphi Museum ▶

VISITING THE DELPHI MUSEUM

I. ANTI – CHAMBER. Ascending the stairs to the right of the main entrance, where the ticket booth can also be found, the visitor will first encounter two rare finds of the excavations in Delphi, which will bring to mind the renowned Delphic symbols and emblems:

● the Omphalos (navel-stone) (3), which is related to the myth of the navel of the Earth at Delphi. It is a sculpted marble copy of the Hellenistic or Roman times, and was dug out near the Temple of Apollo,

● the Tripod with the cauldron (7th century B.C.) which is an imitation of the prophetic tripod of Pythia and also a common offering to Delphi.

To the left, in the passageway, one sees the fragments of a bas-relief of the Herculian contests from the forestage of the theatre (1st century A.D.)

II. ROOM OF THE CERAMICS AND SMALL BRONZE FINDS. It is found in the passageway of the anti-chamber above the stairs. It contains, in 8 showcases, collections of ceramics and other clay objects, as well as numerous other small metal finds such as statuettes, tools, weapons, utensils and jewellery dating from the historic period (43). Some select pieces are found in other rooms, as well as the pre-historic ones, which are found in the last room (XV). Noticeable are the geometric, proto-Corinthian and Corinthian vases, the animal figurines, as well as the bronze reliefs of Eurestheas and Heracles, and Ulysses escaping from the cave of Cyclops tied under a ram (44).

III. ROOM OF THE SHIELDS. Entrance is made from the anti-chamber. Here are displayed rare finds from the beginning of the Oracle's acme (8th - 7th century B.C.), such as a round bronze warrior's shield, offertory decorated shields of Cretan origin, a marble "periranterion" (basin) (620 B.C.) with early samples of upright female statuettes around its base, a bronze griffin (42) of Oriental influences, a delicate small bronze "kouros" (640-620 B.C.) of "Daedalic" style with assimilated foreign influences which foreshadows the characteristics of the large marble "kouroi".

IV. ROOM OF THE KOUROI. It is found opposite the entrance. Here can be seen two similar large "kouroi", Cleovis and Biton (10), which are two of the first examples of the monumental Doric sculpture (600 B.C.), a small bronze "kouros" (41), five sculptured metopes (11) from the Treasury of the Sikyonians with mythical scenes such as the Argonautic Expedition, (the ship Argo), the rape of Europe by Zeus in the form of a bull, the cattlestealing Dioskouroi, Kastor and Pollux, and the Apharidai, Idas and Lyngeus (11), the hunt of the Kalydonian boar (16), and Frixos and Elli on the ram with golden fleece, first witnesses of purely Greek art with remarkable Doric composition and movement (560 B.C.).

V. ROOM OF THE NEW COLLECTION OF WORKS IN IVORY AND GOLD. It is found at the right-hand far end of the room of the "Kouroi". Here can be found unique gold-plated ivory finds (49-54), fragments of two chryselephantine statues, probably of Apollo (54) and Artemis (52), the silverplated bull (55-56), Ionic works (6th century B.C.) which give another dimension to the Greek art in precious metals, a small bronze incense-burner, the "enveiled girl with the censer" (45), two gold plates with decorations (49), several small objects in gold (50,51,53) and other secondary collections.

VI. ROOM OF THE SIPHNIAN TREASURY. Returning to the Room of the Shields and to the left, we find this large room of Archaic sculpture of the Delphi

Museum with incomparable inspiration, and a variety of works of Ionic art (6th century B.C.); a large marble Sphinx (13) which is an offering of the Naxians (570 B.C.), a Caryatid (15) and sculptures, pediment and friezes from the Siphnian Treasury – the quarrel between Heracles and Apollo for the prophetic tripod (22), an assembly of Gods at the Olympus who watch a battle of the Trojan War (24-25), a Homeric duel (23), a battle of Gods against Giants ("Gigantomachy") (19-20) – all representative works of mature Archaic art (535 B.C.).

VII. ROOM OF THE ATHENIAN TREASURY. Entrance is made from the room of the Shields. Here are found metopes from the Treasury of the Athenians with sculpted scenes of the contests of Heracles and Theseus (14,17) works of Attic art (485 B.C.).

VIII and IX. ROOMS OF THE TEMPLE OF APOLLO. Here are displayed sculptures from the Archaic Temple, such as the "arrival of Apollo at Delphi", a marble pediment (21). Here are also the epigraphs with the "Delphic Hymn" with incised musical notation interposed between the lyrics and giving us unique examples of ancient Greek music.

X, XI and XII. ROOMS OF THE SEPULCHRALS, ALTAR AND THOLOS. These are three continuous rooms between the Archaic and the monumental sculptures, of the 4th century B.C. Here can be found the stele of an athlete (29), the marble Altar (48), a small statue of Nike (Victory) (31), as well as a reconstructed part of the Tholos (6), together with metopes and other sculptural and architectural parts of the Tholos.

XIII. ROOM OF AGIAS. Here are found the statue of the athlete Agias (32) which associates the Classical and Hellenistic periods, as well as other statues from the monument of Daochos (330 B.C.), the column with Three dancers (30), which is an original marble (335 B.C.) composition continuing the classical tradition, the Head of Dionysos (38) and the statue of a philosopher (33).

XIV. ROOM OF THE CHARIOTEER. This room exclusively harbours the famous bronze Charioteer of Delphi (470 B.C.), one of the few original works of the Classical Period which have survived (26-28), and the fantastic white Attic Kylix (47) with the illustration of Apollo libating.

XV. ROOM OF ANTINOOS. This last room where the exit stairs are located, accomodates the collections of ceramics from the Prehistoric period (3rd and 2nd millenia B.C.), Mycenean idols of the Φ and Ψ types, and ceramics from the first worshippings at Delphi (13th century B.C.). There are also found collections from the Corycean cave of Parnassus, as well as sculptures from the Greco-Roman period – a philosopher's bust (39), the "smiling child" (36), the head of a statue of magnificent art (40) (2nd century B.C.) and the small statue of a child holding a goose (33). Finally, there can be found the stele of Ploutarch and the statue of Antinoos, (2nd century A.D.) with the deep melancholic expression along the lines of the face (37) which indicates the end of ancient art.

● In front of the Museum have been transferred a mosaic floor from an early Christian church of Delphi (5th century A.D.), a sarcophagus with engraved scenes from the hunt of Meleagros, bas-reliefs from the stele of Aemilius Paulus (Battle of Pydna), and various sculptures and epigraphs from Delphi.

● The numerals on the ground-plan of the rooms of the Museum, and the exhibits in the Museum and on the map with the reconstuction of Delphi relay to the text and the pictures of this book.

LIST OF ILLUSTRATIONS

DELPHI AT THE BEGINNING OF THE 19th CENTURY. *Engraving printed in 1804. About a century later the remains of Delphi were discovered under these houses.*

*THE REMAINS OF DELPHI.
Buried for centuries the remains
of ancient Delphi came to light
during the excavations of 1892-
1903. In the centre of the enclo-
sure of the Sanctuary of Apollo
(right), stood the Temple of Apollo where the Pythia delivered the
oracles for more than a mille-
nium. In the South-East extremi-
ty of the sanctuary is the Sacred
Way which led to the Temple of
Apollo. View from the Phaedriades.*

THE PHAEDRIADES – THE CASTALIAN SPRING. The steep rocks of the Phaedriades rising above the sanctuary of Apollo (left). Between them, the cleft with the Castalian Spring. The famous "speaking water" flows from the bowels of the hewn rock (below), still bringing a fading cry from the depths of the far-gone past.

DELPHI – THE NAVEL OF THE EARTH.

At the foot of Mt Parnassus, below the rocks of the Phaedriades, Delphi spreads out in its splendid natural setting. Opposite is the mount Kirphis ; at the bottom of the impressive steep ravine, the Pleistos river in the deep valley widening out into the Crissaean plain which extends to the bay of Itea ; in the background is the gulf of Corinth and the crest of the Peloponnese mountain range. Legend has it that here was the centre of the world, the "Omphalos" (navel) of the Earth ; a conical stone shows the place where two eagles released by Zeus from two opposed points of the universe, met. Below: The Omphalos (navel) of Delphi- the symbol which is usually connected with the legend of the «navel of the Earth» at Delphi. This was found during the excavations near the Temple of Apollo. Two golden eagles may have stood on this conical marble stone. The Omphalos can be seen in the anti-chamber of the Delphi Museum.

THE ENTRANCE TO THE TEMPLE OF APOLLO – THE SACRED WAY. The entrance of the Temple of Apollo (below), reached by the Sacred Way (right), bordered on each side by numerous offerings, statues and monuments. In the centre, the Athenian Treasury and right, the columns from the Stoa of the Athenians.

5

THE ROUND TEMPLE THOLOS – THE POLYGO-
NAL WALL. *Great architectural monuments were revealed
by the excavations at Delphi and among them rises impres-
sively the round temple Tholos in the sanctuary of
Athena (Pronaia) and the large Polygonal Wall which bisects
horizontally the centre of the sanctuary of Apollo.*
*The Tholos (left) dating to the 4th century. Its function is still
unknown. With its three doric columns (restored) it rises in
the centre of a magical landscape, at Marmaria.*
*The Polygonal Wall (below) dating to the 6th century B.C.
It was built to support the terrace of the Temple of Apollo. A-
bout eight hundred inscriptions are carved on this wall.*

*HE THEATRE AND THE STADIUM OF DELPHI. Lyric, dramatic and athletic contests
alled the Pythia Games where held every four years in the Theatre and the Stadium near the
emple of Apollo, the religious centre. They were as important as the Olympic Games. The Thea-
e, dating back to the 5th century B.C. restored later on, seated 5000. The Stadium also dating
ack to the 5th century B.C., was provided with stone seats in the 2nd century A.D., when the arch
f triumph was added. It seated 7000. The Theatre and the Stadium are still in good repair.*

THE BASE OF THE GOLDEN TRIPOD OF PLATAEA – THE TEMPLE OF APOLLO. On the last bend of the Sacred Way to the Temple of Apollo, is the circular stone base which supported the golden tripod, offered by the Greeks after the victory against the Persians at the Battle of Plataea, in 479 B.C. On the right, the East facade of the Temple of Apollo. The ruins

we can see today are those of the temple completed in 329 B.C. The two earlier temples were destroyed twice, in 548 B.C. and in 373 B.C. The columns of the temple and the stele (right) which
supported the mounted statue of Prussias II, King of Bithynia, have been restored. In the background is the crest of Kirphis, foot-hill of Helicon, the mount of the Muses.

THE ROCK OF SIBYL – THE TREASURY OF THE ATHENIANS. In the middle section of the Sacred Way dominate the "rock of Sibyl" and the Athenian Treasury. From this rock (left) the mythic Sibyl of Delphi delivered her oracles. The Treasury of the Athenians

(right) was built in the early 5th century B.C. in the form of a small Doric temple. It housed the-offerings of the city of Athens. It was rebuilt in 1903-1906. The metopes of the treasury, depicting the exploits of Theseus and Heracles, are copies of the originals which are in the Delphi Museum (fig. 14,17).

Αγγλικά

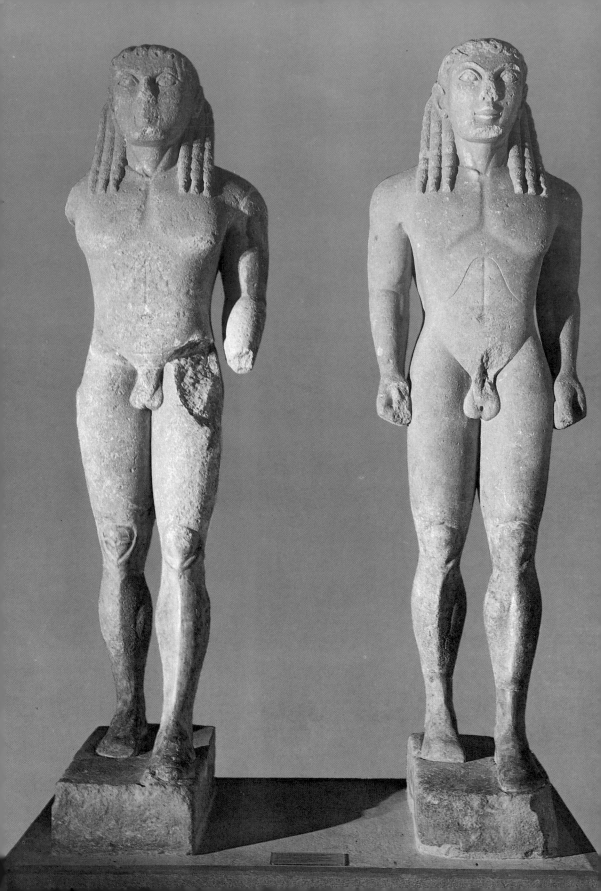

10. THE TWO SIMILAR KOUROI known as Kleobis and Biton. These archaic statues are amongst the earliest large-scale works of Greek sculpture. They are made of marble and are more than two metres high. One of the statues is signed by (Poly?)medes, the Argive sculptor, who probably carved both ot them. About 600 B.C.

11. METOPE FROM THE SIKYONIAN TREASURY. One of the first expressions of Greek art with the characteristic stiffness of movement of the Doric order. This relief represents a mythical scene with the heroes Dioskouroi. About 560 B.C.

*12. WINGED VICTORY (NIKE). Acroterion from the pediment of the archaic
Temple of Apollo. About 510 B.C.*
*13. LARGE MARBLE SPHINX. These mysterious fabulous creatures with
their unworldly expression and smile were popular in archaic art. The Sphinx
with its raised wings is 2.50m. high and must have been most impressive, set up
on an Ionic column approximately ten metres high. It was dedicated by the
Naxians. About 570 B.C.*

12   13

14. THESEUS AND ANTIOPE, QUEEN OF THE AMAZONS. Metope from the Athenian Treasury. This composition full fo sensitivity depicts the bellicose queen of the Amazons following Theseus with her head bent not in submission but in obedience to the voice of her heart. About 490-485 B.C.

15. CARYATID. Marble statue of maiden (kore) in place of a column. This and another similar statue which has disappeared replaced the two columns at the façade of the Siphnian Treasury. About 525 B.C.

15

THREE ARCHITECTURAL SCULPTURES (fig. 16-17-18) depicting the development in archaic art in the 6th century B.C. They belonged to the carved decoration of three Treasuries and come from different workshops : Sikyon, Cyclades and Athens.
16. THE KALYDONIAN BOAR. Metope of porous stone, from the Sikyonian Treasury, depicting the savage boar which was hunted by famous heroes of Greek mythology. About 560 B.C.
17. HERACLES TAMING THE STAG OF CERYNEIA. The hero is returning from a year hunting the mythical stag at Mycenae, to accomplish his third labour. Metope from the Athenian Treasury. About 490-485 B.C.
18. FOUR-HORSE CHAPIOT BEFORE AN ALTAR. Fragment from the South frieze of the Siphnian Treasury. About 525 B.C.

16   18

17

19-20. COMBAT OF GODS AND GIANTS : "GIGANTOMACHY". The North frieze of the Siph-
nian Treasury with the stormy scenes representing the battle of the gods of Olympus against the
giants who sought their power. Participants in the mythical scene are (above, from the left to the
right) Heracles, Kybele riding a chariot drawn by lions, Apollo, Artemis, and (below) Hera, Athena,

Ares, Hermes and Poseidon. The giants who sprang from drops of Uranos blood which fell on the earth after Kronos had dethroned and wounded him, are shown armed with helmets, shields and spears. About 525 B.C.

22

TWO ARCHAIC PEDIMENTS (fig. 21-22)

21. East pediment of the archaic Temple of Apollo ; The sculptures of the group depict Apollo's arrival at Delphi and the welcome given him by King Delphos. About 510 B.C.
22. East pediment of the Siphnian Treasury; The scene is the quarrel of Apollo (left) and Heracles (right) over the Delphic tripod. Zeus stands between restraining them. About 525 B.C.

23-24-25. *DUEL AT TROY—GODS IN COUNCIL AT OLYMPUS. The Eastern frieze of the Siphnian Treasury depicts an episode of the Trojan War, the duel between Hektor (left) and Menelaus (right) before the walls of Troy. The two heroes fought over the dead body of Sarpedon, son of Zeus. They are followed respectively by Aeneas and Glaucos, Ajax and Automedon. The Olympian gods (below), divided into two camps, look on. On the left Ares, Aphrodite,*

Artemis, Apollo are for the Trojans, Zeus on his throne, and in front of him Athena, Hera and De-
meter are for the Greeks. The frieze of the Homeric battle as well as that of the battle of the giants
(fig. 16-17), with the thickly populated compositions, full mouvement, presaged the great sculptures
of the Parthenon after a century. They were on the most seen side of the Siphnian Treasury, facing
the Sacred Way, and were thus visible by those going to the Temple of Apollo. About 525 B.C.

26-27-28. THE CHARIOTEER.
Life-size bronze statue of a young
charioteer who drove a four-horse
chariot (only the legs and the tails of
the horses remain) to victory in the
Pythia Games. It is one of the few sur-
viving masterpieces of ancient Greek
art; it is the most famous work in the
Delphi Museum. Below and right:
Details from the body and the face of
the Charioteer, with the impression
of nobility partly due to the expres-
sion of the eyes made of coloured
stones. About 470 B.C.

29. *FUNERARY STELE OF AN ATHLETE. Relief from the mid 5th century B.C.*
30. *THE THREE DANCERS. Group in marble with three girls in high-relief who appear to be dancing on a column capital. It supported a tripod in the sanctuary at Delphi. An original unique work, it continues the classical tradition. About 335 - 325 B.C.*

30

31. NIKE (VICTORY). Skillfully worked marble acroterion. It comes from the sculptures of the sanctuary of Athena (Pronaia) at Marmaria. About 370 B.C.

32. AGIAS. Original work in marble, of the first Thessalian to win the pankration (boxing and wrestling competition) at the Olympic Games; his personality is realistically and vividly rendered. This is another creation of the century following the classical period and it sums up the admirable development of Hellenistic art. The statue belongs to a group dedicated by Daochos at Delphi. About 330 B.C.

31 32

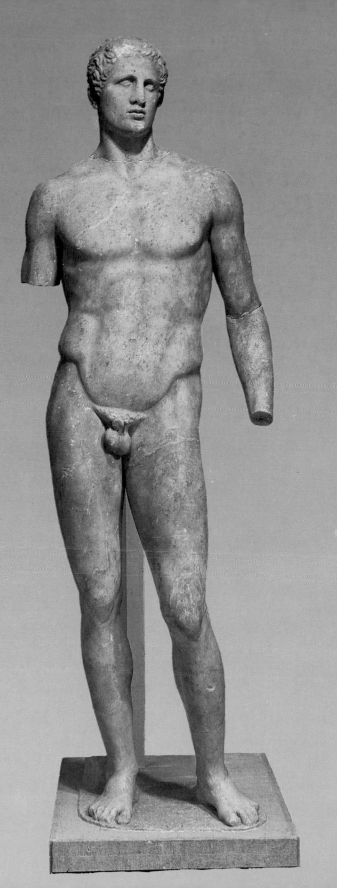

33. A STATUE OF A CHILD holding a goose, offering to Apollo. Late 3rd century B.C.
34. SISYPHUS I. Statue in marble which belongs to a monument dedicated by Daochos at Delphi. About 330 B.C.
35. STATUE OF A PHILOSOPHER (?) Original work in marble from the Hellenistic period. About 280 B.C.

33 34 35

36. THE SMILING CHILD. *Marble statue of a small girl. Her expressive face is brightened by a smile. Early 3rd century B.C.*

37. ANTINOOS. *Original sculpture in marble with the expression of deep melancholy which marked the final phase of Greek art. The statue was dedicated at Delphi after the emperor Hadrian had conferred divine honours on his young favourite who had drowned in the Nile. About 128 A.D.*

36 37

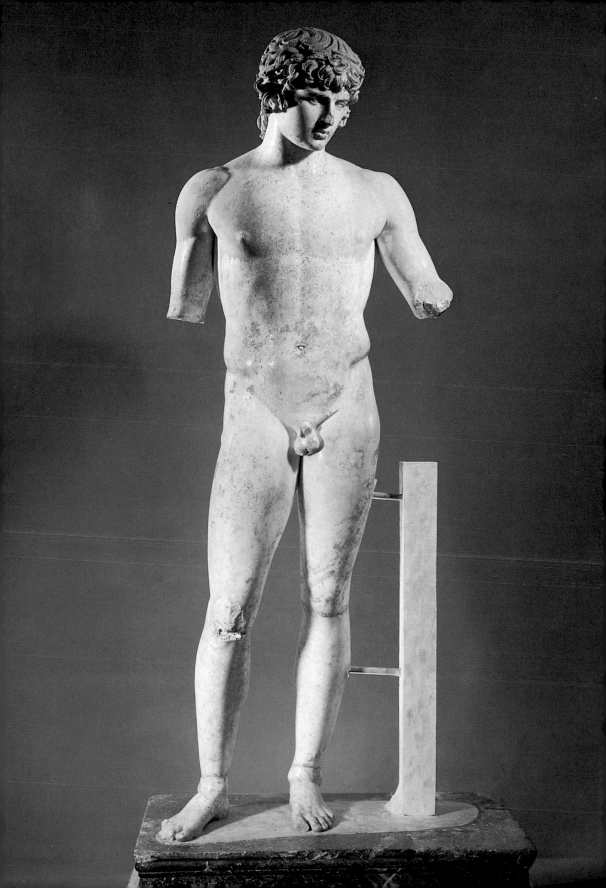

38. HEAD OF DIONYSOS. It comes from the sculptured group of the pediment of the temple of Apollo. 4th century B.C.
39. BUST OF A PHILOSOPHER. This comes from a stele (hermes) of the 2nd century A.D.
40. HEAD FROM A STATUE. This head probably belongs to the statue of a Roman hypate. Late 2nd century B.C.

38 39 40

SMALL BRONZES FROM THE DELPHI MUSEUM (fig. 41-45).

41. *Bronze statuette of Kouros. 6th cen.B.C.*
42. *Bronze griffin. 6th cen.B.C.*
43. *Handle of a bronze cauldron. 6th cen.B.C.*
44. *Odysseus (Ulysses) tied under the ram escapes from the cave of Cyclops. Bronze relief. 6th century B.C.*
45. *Bronze incense-burner. A girl wearing a peplos (type of dress), holding an incense-burner in her upraised hands. This original work is one of the finest small-scale classical bronze sculptures. About 450 B.C.*

45

PAINTED POTTERY FROM DELPHI MUSEUM *(fig. 46-47)*
46. Attic funerary vase (lecythe). It represents a winged Victory (Nike) making a libation in front of the altar. Middle 5th century B.C.

47. The inside of a cup (kylix) which had handles, showing Apollo with his head laurel-crowned pouring a libation. In his left hand he holds his lyre, exactly drawn. The painting is on a white ground. About 470 B.C.

THE NEW COLLECTION

OF WORKS IN IVORY AND GOLD

FROM DELPHI MUSEUM (fig. 49-56).

48. MARBLE ALTAR with sculptural decoration. Copy, from the 2nd century B.C.

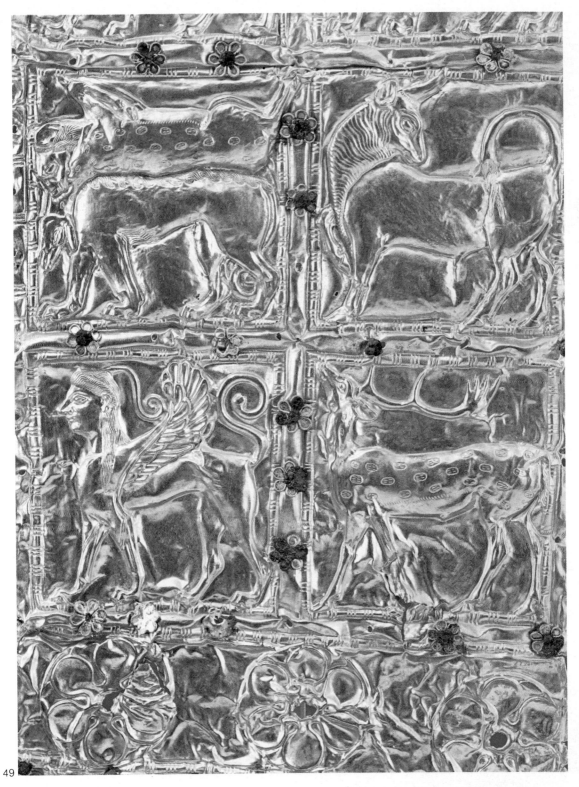

49

49. Detail from two plates in gold with animals and fabulous creatures. 6th cen.B.C.

50-51. *GOLD ROSETTE AND GRIFFIN. These admirable pieces were found among the «treasury of Delphi» in a pit. 6th century B.C.*
52. *HEAD OF THE STATUE OF A GODDESS IN GOLD AND IVORY, probably of Artemis. 6th century B.C.*

50 51

53. GOLD LIONS HEAD from a necklace. 6th century.B.C.
54. HEAD OF AN IVORY AND GOLD STATUE, probably of Apollo. 6th century.B.C.

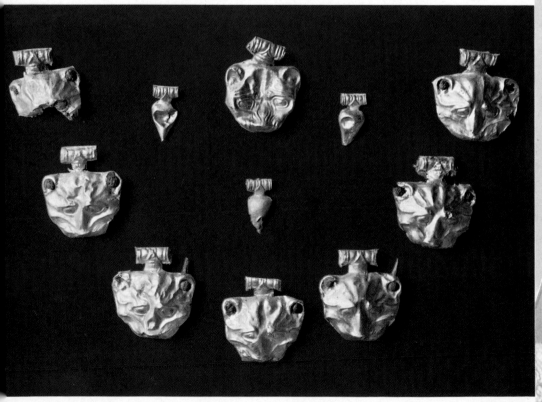

53 54

55. *THE SILVER BULL. Lifesize work made out of silver sheets with gilding on the head and elsewhere, gives another aspect of Greek artistry in precious metals. This work is unrivalled, a unique masterpiece of Ionian work dedicated at Delphi in the mid-6th century B.C.*

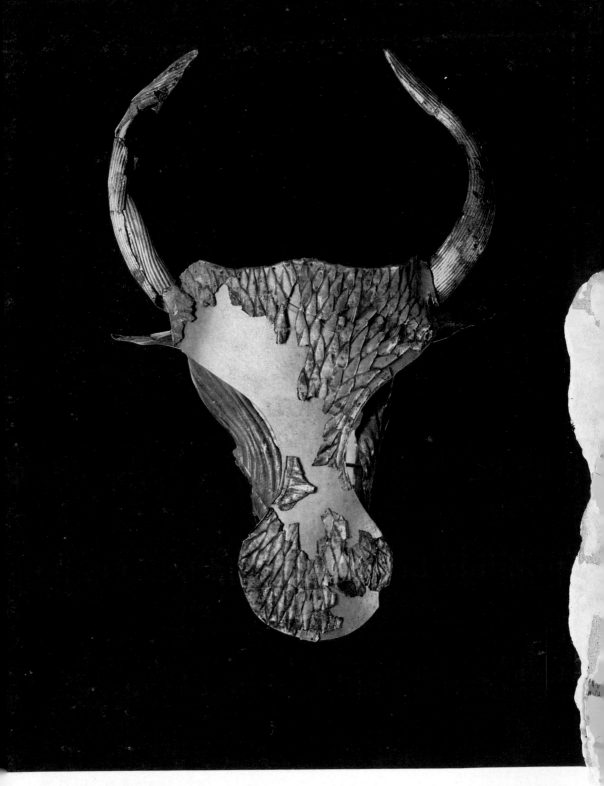

56. THE HEAD OF THE SILVER BULL WITH GILT ORNAMENTATION :
A detail which is in itself a masterpiece. 6th century B.C.